Literary and Philosophical Society of Liverpool

Suggestions Offered on the Part of the Literary and Philosophical Society of Liverpool,

To Members of the Mercantile Marine...

Literary and Philosophical Society of Liverpool

Suggestions Offered on the Part of the Literary and Philosophical Society of Liverpool,
To Members of the Mercantile Marine...

ISBN/EAN: 9783337069834

Printed in Europe, USA, Canada, Australia, Japan

Cover: Foto ©Thomas Meinert / pixelio.de

More available books at **www.hansebooks.com**

Suggestions

OFFERED ON THE PART OF THE

LITERARY AND PHILOSOPHICAL SOCIETY

OF LIVERPOOL,

TO MEMBERS OF THE MERCANTILE MARINE,

WHO MAY BE DESIROUS OF USING THE ADVANTAGES THEY ENJOY

For the Promotion of Science,

IN

FURTHERANCE OF ZOOLOGY.

LIVERPOOL:

PRINTED FOR THE SOCIETY,

BY T. BRAKELL, 7, COOK STREET.

1862.

Suggestions*

OFFERED ON THE PART OF THE

LITERARY AND PHILOSOPHICAL SOCIETY

OF LIVERPOOL,

TO MEMBERS OF THE MERCANTILE MARINE,

Who may be desirous of using the advantages they enjoy for the promotion of Science, in furtherance of Zoology.

INTRODUCTION.

THE science of Natural History necessitates two methods of investigation. One method is the study of the external and internal characters of natural objects, their peculiarities, resemblances and differences. The other is the study of their manners and habits; the conditions under which they are found; and their distribution over the earth and seas.

The first method requires *closet* study, and may be most effectually pursued by the stay-at-home naturalist; the second can only be followed where the living objects themselves are to be found. Given the supply of specimens, the one may be carried on within the walls of a Museum; the other can only

---

* On the proposal of the Secretary, and in furtherance of the views developed in the paper at page 46, " On the Opportunities of advancing Science enjoyed by the Mercantile Marine," a sub-committee was appointed to draw up some hints which might be useful to such merchant officers as were willing to make good use of their advantages for promoting Zoological investigation. The sub-committee consisted of Dr. Collingwood, Mr. T. J. Moore and Dr. Walker. To these were subsequently added the Rev. H. H. Higgins and Mr. I. Byerley. To Mr. Moore was intrusted the task of preparing a paper to be put into the hands of such persons as were likely to avail themselves of such hints, and the following suggestions were adopted by the Committee, and ordered to be printed in an Appendix, and further circulated among Members of the Mercantile Marine.

be completely accomplished by *observation* in every land and every sea, at every season, and during many years.

The second method *may* be independent of the first, but followers of the first are almost entirely dependent for their very material on the contributions made by the followers of the second, or by less intelligent providers of specimens. Unquestionably every student should cultivate both methods as far as circumstances permit, but in an inverse proportion to his advantages for pursuing one, will generally be his facilities for following the other.

The closet student with his books and microscopes and other advantages, can profit to the fullest extent by the labours of his predecessors and contemporaries. He can carry on investigations into new fields of discovery and bring to light previously hidden laws of structure or even of development, —studies requiring long and close application and the examination and comparison of specimens from widely distant parts of the world. As a rule *he* must limit his acquaintance with living nature to the inhabitants of his native country, to hurried observations of those met with in a brief summer tour, or to the " cabined, cribbed, confined" specimens in a menagerie or aquarium.

The field or ocean naturalist on the other hand, if devoting himself exclusively to his science, revels in the contemplation of the habits, manners and instincts of created beings in any and every part of the world ; yet if a collector, and an ardent one, he cannot attain such a close acquaintance with the internal structure, or even with the development, of anything like the number of animals of widely different kinds and widely distant countries as can his brother of the closet. How much less can he do so if from professional or other duties he is prevented from devoting more than a portion of his time to the study of nature ! Yet though the closet and field naturalists cannot be independent of each other, each class may derive many and great benefits from the observations and labours of the other. Owen could not have studied so long and so closely as he has done the bony frame-work of animals, if he must himself have gone to New Zealand and sought for that single and very imperfect bone from which, being sent to him, he first made known the fact of a race of birds of gigantic size and remarkable character having formerly existed in those remote islands, and pointed out so accurately the kind of bird it must have been, that subsequently, when bones of other parts in considerable numbers, and ultimately a complete skeleton, were discovered and brought to England, his deductions were fully and incontestably proved.*

On the other hand, had the discoverer of this bone himself sought to solve the problem of the kind of animal to which it had belonged, it would have required vast research, in comparing various parts of skeletons of very various kinds, and a long study of the value and significance of seemingly trifling modifications of form and structure, to have approximated at all to a solution of the question.

Take another illustration. Everybody has seen, not only in museums and the shops of dealers, but on the mantel-piece and side-table, the shells of the Pearly Nautilus, shells which for beauty of lustre and elegance of form are unsurpassed; while their chambered structure evinces important differences in the living inhabitants from those of all other shells. These shells are so plentiful as to be sold for a few shillings only; and two or three species are known to exist; while the *extinct species*, of which fossil remains are found, often very perfect and beautiful, may be counted by hundreds. Yet though the recent shells have been long known and im-

---

* The bone referred to was a thigh bone broken off at both ends, fully described and figured in the Transactions of the Zoological Society of London, for 1839. Subsequently several distinct species have been made out by Professor Owen from bones collected in New Zealand, all fully described in later volumes of the same publication.

ported in such abundance, the *animals* which formed them remained almost unknown to naturalists until the year 1829. Previously, the animal had only been very imperfectly figured, and still more imperfectly described, by a Dutch naturalist in the 18th century, who had seen a living example. Cuvier never saw a specimen of the animal, though greatly desiring to do so. He prophetically said it would never gladden his eyes, and they were closed in death, though but only a few days (?) when the first specimen reaching Europe was sent to Paris for his inspection. Subsequent critical examination served to establish the existence of a character of the highest importance, that of the possession by the Nautilus family of double the number of gills found in any other family of the class of animals to which it belongs, thus placing in a still stronger light the difference in structure and relationships of the numberless fossil species, for long periods, so abundant upon the earth.

Both these notable instances show how greatly even the most advanced closet student depends for most important material upon those who may be called, for distinction's sake, *field naturalists*; how greatly the latter may aid the former; with what a rich return in knowledge they may be repaid; and what a flood of light may result from the combined labours of both.

Again, the natural history of any class of animals cannot be fully known until all the different species thereof are ascertained; how long each species has existed on the earth or in the waters; how widely it is distributed through the same; its habits, whether migratory or stationary, solitary or gregarious; its mode of reproduction and course of development; its seasonal and other changes; its food and mode of obtaining it; its haunts; its powers of offence or defence; the length of life of individuals; and numerous other particulars. Only in proportion as these various facts are correctly ascertained of *individual species*, is it possible to arrive at correct conclusions relating to any larger group of animals, and to elucidate the great laws of animated nature. Much has already been done in this direction, but very, very much more remains to be accomplished.

The very first step and the foundation of all subsequent generalizations is the *correct determination of the different kinds*, or *species*, of animals;—and this is by no means so easy a task as might at first be supposed. Some species approximate to others so closely as to require careful examination to distinguish them : others vary so much as to necessitate the comparison of many specimens before all their points of difference can be ascertained. Among large animals species may generally be recognized without much difficulty; but very frequently, and particularly among minute objects, the closest examination and comparison with descriptions and drawings are necessary; while often the assistance of students of the particular tribe of objects must be sought as indispensable.

Scarcely inferior in importance to science is the *knowledge of the range of species*, to what extent, great or small, they are distributed over earth or seas. Indeed Agassiz, one of the greatest Naturalists of this or any other age, goes so far as to assert that " every new fact relating to the geographical distribution of well known species is as important to science as the discovery of a new species. Could we only know the range of a single animal as accurately as Alphonse de Candolle has determined that of many species of plants, we might begin a new era in Zoology. It is greatly to be regretted, that in most works containing the scientific results of explorations of distant countries, only new species are described, when the mere enumeration of those already known might have added invaluable information respecting their geographical distribution. The carelessness with which some naturalists distinguish species, merely because they are found in distant regions, without even attempting to secure specimens for comparison, is a perpetual source of erroneous conclusions in the study of the geographical distribution of organised beings, not less detrimental to the progress of science than the readiness of others to consider as identical, animals and plants which may resemble each other closely, without paying the least regard to their distinct origin, and without even pointing out the differences they perceive between specimens from different parts of the world. The perfect indentity of animals and plants living in very remote parts of the globe has so often been ascertained, and it is also so well known how closely species may be allied, and yet differ in all the essential relations which characterize species, that such loose investigations are no longer justifiable."

It is important to observe that in cases of close identity, real or apparent, between animals, accurate observation of their respective habits and other circumstances connected with their life-history will frequently materially assist to a right conclusion.

From the foregoing observations the following conclusions may be drawn :—That the knowledge of Natural History may be largely promoted by those "who go down to the sea in ships," by the collecting of specimens, whereby new kinds of animals may occasionally be obtained; by recording the time when, and places where they occur, thus adding to our knowledge of their distribution; by observing their habits and mode of life, thus filling up many a blank page in the history of animated beings, and often assisting materially in elucidating their true relations to other animals; while occasionally it may happen that specimens, or information relative to habits, may be preserved, of animals which may, in no long time, become extinct, as have several large species of birds during the last 20 years, as the great Auk, (probably) the Philip Island Parrot, the Didunculus, &c., and perhaps the Moa of New Zealand.

Perfect certainty regarding species, however, is of the utmost importance. On this one point everything else will turn. It is, in fact, the *exact determination of the thing spoken of;* and unless that determination be correct, any record of occurrence or notice of habits will be vitiated. Astronomical observations, however correctly taken or elaborately worked up, would be of little value, if there were any doubt as to the particular star observed ; so of any notes of species, if those species be incorrectly named ; *unless* indeed, examples of the species accompany the notes.

BUT *if this latter be the case, if examples accompany the notes, all the responsibility for the correct naming of species may be at once transferred to others better placed for determining them, either by access to rare or costly books, or by their familiarity with the particular tribe of animals to which they belong.*

We come then briefly to this :—That large and often important additions may be made to Zoological knowledge by members of the Mercantile Marine, by recording places of occurence, and notes of habits, of such living objects as may come under their observation ; but that to be of service, the animals to which they relate must be determined with the *strictest accuracy,* (by no means an easy matter,) or *be accompanied by specimens of the objects spoken of,* which will at once remove the difficulty. Of course the acquisition of specimens is of itself a great object to Museums, Collectors, and Students. It is here, however, considered subordinate to the acquisition of a knowledge of their life-history,—but it will in fact be found to be almost absolutely necessary to the imparting of that knowledge.

Let us suppose the case of a Merchant-Captain, or Officer, really desirous of doing something, however trifling, to add to our scientific knowledge. A land bird alights exhausted on the rigging of his ship, far out at sea—unless the bird be

captured and preserved, to be produced along with the statement of its occurence, that statement would be of little value,
unless the observer were an accomplished ornithologist, and
had actually handled the bird in order closely to examine and
determine it. Suppose a Squid or a Cuttle Fish be obtained.
The fact (with the lat. and long.,) would be worth recording,
but not unless the specimen were preserved also, unless the
observer were a student of this particular class of animals,
and knew, or could determine from his books, the exact
species ; for the known kinds of these animals are numerous,
while many yet doubtless remain unknown.

So with Fish, with Crabs, Shells, and all other animals;
unless the observer be a student of these particular kinds of
animals, and able of his own direct knowledge, or from his
general acquaintance with the subject, authoritatively to determine the species from well selected and often rare and
costly books, there and then on board, his notices of them
would be of little value, *unless accompanied by actual specimens of the things spoken of.* But *if* so accompanied, so
simple a thing as a reference to them by a numbered label,
would at once save him from all trouble and anxiety on this
score, leaving it to his arrival at port, to settle these points by
the aid of others, or to leave *that* portion of the business
entirely in their hands. This bringing home of specimens in
elucidation of notes and observations need not be a never-
ending matter. Once done, it may not, for that particular
kind, need repetition. One or more preserved examples of a
kind may be kept by the Collector, which once named may
serve for future references, or his observation will become
quickened, enabling him to appreciate and retain a firm
recollection of the particular points of specific distinction.
Very many specimens of high scientific interest, may be
preserved and packed in such a way as to be readily accessible
for reference, without occupying more space, than may easily

be spared, even where room is so much an object, as on board ship. There are of course, small shells, crustacea, and other objects of little bulk.

It only remains therefore, to point out the less obvious methods of collecting; the chief methods of preservation; the most serviceable material for both, and to direct those who are desirous of further information to some of the most useful works of reference.

MAMMALIA.

Under the term mammalia are comprised all those animals which suckle their young, including not only quadrupeds, ordinarily so called, but also the seals and the more fish-like creatures of the whale and dolphin kinds. These aquatic animals are rare in museums, and many species are very imperfectly known. Instances of their being met with are well worth recording, and specimens should be preserved whenever practicable. When it may be inconvenient to save the skin or skeleton, the skull should at any rate be secured. Notes of the date and place of capture, and whether occurring singly or in shoals, as well as of any other circumstances that may be noticed, should be recorded in a note-book at the time, or be written on a label and attached to the specimen.

Many of these marine forms are found only in high latitudes, and out of the general course of trading vessels. Such specimens as may be met with should be made the most of. The dugongs of the Indian seas and the coast of Australia are great desiderata in England; as are also the lamantins of the West coast of Africa, and the manatees of the West Indies and the coasts of Guiana and Demerara.

The skeletons as well as the skins of these are much wanted, and both may be preserved from the same creature. There is but little skill required in either operation. *The skin* may easily be taken off the carcase : as much as possible of the flesh and

blubber should be removed, and a mixture of one-third salt
and two-thirds alum rubbed all over the fleshy side of the skin.
When this has been well done, place the skin in a barrel
with a quantity of the alum and salt above and below it, as
well as between all the folds. Turn it and rub it with the salt
and alum daily for four or five days, according to the size of
the animal, in order to ensure its being well cured. After
lying two or three weeks in the brine thus produced, it may
be taken out, sprinkled with more salt and alum, and packed
like a wet hide; or if more convenient, it may be dried by
exposure to the air. When alum is not to be had, salt alone
may be used.

The above method is applicable to large skins of all kinds.

To preserve *the skeleton*, cut off all the flesh from the bones,
but without separating them more than is necessary. Tie
them carefully in coarse strong canvas or sacking, and tow
them after the vessel, or otherwise soak them till the remaining
flesh has rotted off. They should be examined occasionally, in
order to tie up in separate bags the small bones of each limb,
before they become divided and mixed. This is desirable to
save trouble in afterwards sorting them, and to prevent loss.

When the bones are quite clean, white, and free from grease,
they may be dried and stowed away, with a suitable label
annexed. Care should be taken to cut out from the flesh *all*
the bones, including those of the tongue, &c., and vigilance
exercised that none be lost.*

When circumstances prevent either skin or skeleton being
preserved, *the skull* may yet be saved, and, if so, should by
all means be secured. The flesh being removed, it may be
cleaned by towing as directed for skeletons. If notes of the
sex, colors and measurements of the animal can be taken, they

* An admirable skeleton of a half-grown Indian rhinoceros, prepared in the
above manner, may be seen in the Free Public Museum of Liverpool; the skin
of the same animal was also preserved and cured in the manner pointed out
above.

will be of value, especially should the species be rare. A sketch of the relative position of the blow-hole, hump (where it exists) and of the flippers is desirable in the case of rare specimens of the whale and dolphin kinds.

Professor Owen, speaking of the National Museum in a little work lately published by him,* draws special attention to the large marine mammalia, the whales and seals, and strongly urges the securing of specimens, as their rapidly decreasing numbers and more restricted range, owing to the eagerness with which they are pursued and destroyed for commercial purposes, point to their speedy extermination. One of the chief objects of his book is to secure ample space in the British Museum for the proper display of the skins and skeletons of these creatures, not only on behalf of the public, but for "the special student of this least known and most difficult branch of mammalogy."

Land animals of great rarity and interest, such as the gorilla of South West Africa, and the orangs of Borneo and Sumatra, may be *best* preserved as follows :—Lose no time in taking off the skin ; let this be done very carefully. Leave no bones at all in the skin, nor any flesh. Immerse the skin at once in the strongest spirit that can be procured, taking care that it gets well between every fold, and that no part is exposed to the air. To ensure full contact of every part with the spirit, lift up the skin occasionally. If possible, after a day or two, draw off the old spirit, and supply its place with *new*. Absorption into the skin is so great, and evaporation, in such hot climates as these animals are found in, is so rapid, that unless the spirit be renewed, the preservation may not be thoroughly effected. Let the barrel be proportioned to the bulk of the skin, tie the skin in canvas to prevent chafing against the staves; put in as much grass or other light material

* "On the Extent and Aims of a National Museum of Natural History, by Professor Owen. London: Saunders, Otley, and Co. 1862." 8vo. Price 6s.

as will prevent all shaking, and *fill the barrel with spirit to the bung.**

The bones of such animals as the above are too valuable to be left behind. The entire carcase, without separating from it a single bone, may be exposed to ants, or other insect cleansers, if properly secured against more powerful depredators; and when partly eaten by these little creatures, and partly dried by the sun, a semi-mummy, it may be packed in a suitable box, until its arrival at home. This was done with the entire skeleton of the gorilla referred to below, and not a bone was lost or misplaced. The least possible amount of labour suffices for this method of preserving a skeleton.

Animals may be preserved bodily *in spirit*, without any further trouble than making a small incision in the skin of the abdomen to allow the spirit access to the intestines—care being taken that the intestines themselves are not cut; that the spirit be strong; and also that it be, if possible, changed within a short time for fresh spirit. The only limit to the size of the animals thus treated is the quantity of spirit that can be afforded. It is by far the best plan for all small mammalia, such as bats, moles, mice, &c., and really involves very little trouble.

For those who may have opportunities of procuring quadrupeds, and desire to preserve their skins for stuffing, the following directions may be serviceable, though an hour's practical instruction would give a clearer notion of the process than can possibly be obtained without it.

To prepare and preserve Skins of Mammalia.

The animal to be skinned should be placed on its back, and an incision made down the middle of the abdomen, care being

---

* In this manner, a skin of a large gorilla, also in the Liverpool Museum, has been received in a condition leaving nothing to be desired, far surpassing any that have been previously imported. If spirit be not available, salt will be the best substitute.

first taken to divide the hair to the right and left, and then to avoid cutting through the abdominal muscles.

The length of the incision will depend much on the skill of the operator. A novice had better make it from the collar-bone to within a short distance of the vent; as he gains skill, a shorter opening will suffice to enable him to remove the carcase. A small quantity of powdered chalk, or of plaster of Paris, should be at hand, to be used from a pepper-box in dusting over and absorbing the blood whenever it may be troublesome, or endanger the cleanliness of the fur. The skin may then be removed from either side of the body, as far as the fore and hind legs, by a careful use of knife and fingers. The fore legs should be separated from the carcase by cutting between the shoulder-blades and the ribs; and the hind legs, by cutting the integument which binds the head of the thigh-bone to its socket in the hip. Leaving the separated limbs for a time, the operator should continue skinning the body downwards to the tail, the gut being cut through about an inch from the vent, and the tail cut off at the first joint. The skin may then be reversed and separated from the carcase upwards to the neck. Continuing the inversion, the whole of the neck should be skinned as far up as the skull, when, if the head be too large to be drawn within the reversed skin of the neck, as in horned animals, it may be separated from the skull at the atlas or first joint of the vertebræ. The skin should then be turned with the hairy side out, and a fresh longitudinal incision made therein from the chin to a short distance down the throat, in order again to get at the skull, which must be carefully and cleanly skinned down to the lips, taking particular care to cut the ears off close down to the skull, and to avoid cutting the eyelids and lips. Carefully skin the lips to the margin and even beyond, so as to leave as great a portion as possible of the inner skin attached, in order to preserve the natural appearance of the mouth when the animal shall be ultimately stuffed. The incision down the throat, however, should be avoided whenever the head can be skinned and cleansed by drawing it through the neck. This can be done with all except horned animals. The eyes should be removed by pushing them in a forward direction out of their sockets by a flat piece of wood, or the handle of the knife, and cutting the nerve, when they will be displaced without much difficulty. The whole of the flesh, tongue, and brains, should be removed from the skull as cleanly as possible, the last being extracted from the hole at the base of the skull by a small wooden scoop, or by enlarging the hole so as to admit a larger instrument; but this enlargement should be *avoided when possible*, because of the injury it causes to the skull.

The fore and hind legs may then be proceeded with, and should be skinned down to the very hoofs or claws. The flesh should be carefully removed from the bones of the legs, *but on no account should the bones be cut away ;* they should be left attached to the hoof or claws, and all saved as far as the shoulder and the hip. The tail may be skinned by baring the first joint or so, and tying thereto a stout string or cord, fastening it to a beam, and slipping the remaining length out of the skin by means of a cleft stick, with a square surface made to clasp either side of the skinned joint, and smartly pulling the stick to the end of the tail.

The whole skin should now be examined, and all particles of flesh still adhering must be carefully removed. The whole of the inner surface, especially about the lips, eyes, and vent, is to be well and amply smeared over with arsenical soap, or other preservative, if this, the most valuable, be not at hand. The leg bones must be well covered with the preservative, and, after being slightly wrapped round with tow, or other material, to prevent them from adhering to the skin, should be returned within the extremities. The skull, having been well dressed with preservative, should have its cavities slightly filled out with tow, cotton, or other light material, and replaced within the skin. The body may be slightly stuffed out with any light material at hand, and the abdominal incision slightly sewn up. The hair should be well smoothed and cleaned, and any external part of the skin destitute of hair, touched with the preservative. A parchment or card label should be tied to one of the legs, and the date when the animal was killed, locality, native name, &c., recorded thereon. The skin may be carefully laid by in some dry and airy place out of the reach of vermin and insects, and there remain till thoroughly dry, when it may be placed in a box or chest, care being still taken against the access of insects, &c., the box should, therefore, be as air-tight as possible, and some camphor or other drug obnoxious to insects placed therein.

Great care should be taken in all the above processes *not to stretch* the skin, because it is generally impossible after-wards to reduce it to its former size. The *shrinking* of a skin is of little moment, as it can, when damped for stuffing, be easily pulled out to its former size ; but *stretching* should be carefully guarded against.

BIRDS.

In ornithology, members of the Mercantile Marine cannot do better than take every opportunity of securing such land birds as may alight on board their vessels while at sea, and either preserve their skins or put them in spirit, previously making a slight incision in the abdomen, carefully noting the latitude and longitude, and the date. Any information that can be obtained relative to the migrations of birds will be useful. Instances of migratory flocks being seen on the wing at sea would be worth recording; particularly noting the latitude and longitude, the direction of the flight, and the direction and force of the wind. If specimens can be shot and preserved, the value of the observation will be, of course, very greatly increased, as it would put the identity of the species beyond a doubt. Opportunities for collecting eggs and nests of birds will not often fall to the lot of members of the Mercantile Marine, especially as regards land birds. As, however, skins are very much more frequently collected than eggs and nests, the chance of obtaining novelties is proportionally greater, and such opportunities of obtaining them as may occur should be made the most of.

Great circumspection, however, is necessary. For eggs to be of value to the ornithologist, it is necessary to be *certain* of the species to which they belong. In all cases, therefore, where it may be possible to capture one or both of the parent birds, as well as the eggs, it is strongly recommended to do so. So high a value is placed by modern collectors of eggs on correct identification, that no trouble is considered too great which may be found necessary to ascertain with accuracy the parent birds.

Mr. Alfred Newton, one of the most zealous collectors of eggs of the day, gives the following advice on this point in a little pamphlet written by him for the Smithsonian Institution of Washington, and subsequently published by him in England.*

"The most satisfactory, and often the simplest, way of identifying the species to which a nest of eggs, when found, belongs, is to obtain one of the parents by shooting, snaring, or trapping. But it sometimes, in practice, happens that this is found to be difficult, from one cause or another, such as the wary instinct of the birds, or the necessities of his position compelling the traveller to lose no time, or the scarcity of the species making him unwilling to destroy the individuals. In any of these cases, there is nothing to be done but to make as

---

* " Suggestions for forming Collections of Birds' Eggs, by Alfred Newton, M.A. Published by Edward Newman, 9, Devonshire-street, Bishopsgate, London. Price 0d." This little pamphlet is strongly recommended to all those who are disposed to take a special interest in the subject of which it treats.

careful an examination as circumstances will admit, of the precise situation of the nest, the materials of which it is composed (supposing that the collector cannot bring it away with him), and accurately to survey the surrounding locality, to observe by what species it is frequented; all the particulars of which examination and survey should be fully noted down at the earliest opportunity possible. Should, however, either or both the birds be killed, they should be skinned, or at least some characteristic part of each preserved, and duly labelled, to correspond with the inscriptions subsequently put on the eggs, and always with a reference to the collector's journal or note-book, wherein fuller details may be found.

" The collector of eggs is especially warned not to be misled by the mere fact of seeing birds around or near the nests. Many of the crow family (*Corvidæ*), are great eaters of eggs, and mistakes are known to have originated from birds of that kind being seen near nests of which they were certainly not the owners. Others, such as the Titmice (*Paridæ*), though not plunderers, obtain their food by incessantly seeking it, even in the very localities where many species build. It often happens, also, that two different birds have their nests situated very close to one another, and if they be allied species the collector may be easily deceived."

The best method of blowing eggs is to make a *single hole in the side*, and not at either end as is commonly done. The latter method breaks the outline of the egg, and doubles the risk of cracking the shell. The former method answers every purpose, and, when the egg is placed with the hole downwards, there is nothing to offend the eye. The egg may be blown by means of a blow-pipe or a stalk of grass. The hole being being made somewhat larger than the tip of the pipe or stalk, the contents of the shell cannot but escape when air is blown in. A rat-tailed file, with a very sharp point, is a very effectual borer for making the hole in moderate and large-sized eggs ; a brad-awl, sharpened to a point, or a three-cornered needle, will suffice for small ones.

In the very common event of the young bird being more or less advanced towards hatching, considerable care and dexterity will be required in extracting it. Mr. Newton recommends gumming on the side of the shell, one over another, a series of circular pieces of paper (such as would be cut by a punch for gun waddings), and then slit in several places from the circumference half way towards the centre, with a pair of scissors, in order to allow them to be accommodated to the convexity of the egg. When dry, the hole is to be made through these, which will add considerably to the strength of that part of the shell ; and the embryo is to be very carefully cut up and drawn out by skilful manipulation with the most slender knives, hooks, or scissors, that can be procured. The patches of paper can easily be removed by softening them sufficiently in water. Care should always be taken to clean the eggs well out, to rinse them with a little water, and to leave the egg hole downwards until thoroughly dry.

When dry, each egg should be wrapped in a small quantity of cotton wool, or the lightest substitute available, and all out of one nest, packed within the nest, if it be saved, or put together into a chip box. Such box, or nest of eggs, should be most carefully labelled with the place and time of capture ; and the name, native or otherwise, of the parent birds, stating particularly the circumstances warranting the application of the latter, such as " Parent bird shot on the nest, and sent herewith, numbered so-and-so." As the small boxes and nests of eggs accumulate, they should be carefully packed in a box of larger size, and so as to prevent shaking. Wrapping each egg separately is far preferable to putting them in sawdust, sand, grain, or similar material, as by shaking in travelling the eggs get to the top, the sand, &c., to the bottom of the box, and much damage ensues.

The following directions for skinning birds may be useful in the absence of practical lessons :—

To Prepare and Preserve Skins of Birds.

Birds, when shot, should have the mouth and vent stopped up with cotton, wool, or fine grass, and the wounds dusted with powdered chalk, or plaster of Paris, to prevent any discharge of blood, or mucus, from soiling the feathers. These precautions may be repeated when the body is cool enough for skinning. The feathers being carefully divided to the left and right, down to the centre of the under surface of the bird, an incision is to be made from the upper part of the breast to the vent; and the skin on either side separated from the flesh by the fingers, very little aid being required from the knife; the legs should be cut from the trunk at the knee-joint, that is, between the thigh and leg bone in the fleshy part of the leg, and the skin separated from the body as far as the vent and tail, both of which must be cut off at a short distance from their termination. This is, perhaps, the most difficult task in skinning a bird, and considerable care will be necessary. The last joint of the vertebræ supporting the tail may be left attached to the skin to continue its support to the tail feathers, but all the flesh and the oil-gland must be carefully removed. Skin the back upwards till the wings are reached; separate these at their junction with the body, taking especial care here not to cut the skin; tie the mandibles together with a thread passed *very* carefully through the nostrils with a fine needle, so as not to injure the nostrils (which are very delicate, and possess characters of scientific importance), and leave a double thread attached somewhat longer than the neck. Draw out the neck as far as the skull, and skin carefully round this as far as the base of the mandibles, taking care in removing the eyes not to puncture, or otherwise injure, the lids; cut away the tongue and all the flesh from the skull, and scoop out the brain, to do which it may be necessary to remove a small portion of the base of the skull, yet so as not to injure its contour, or lessen its strength. The legs are now to be skinned as far as there is any flesh, which must be removed from the bones, anointed with *arsenical soap or other preservative*, then slightly wrapped with tow or cotton, and returned to their place. In a similar way, the wings must be skinned, except that the flesh from the second joint onward may be removed through a fresh incision on the inner side of the wing instead of drawing out the whole length of the bones. Having dressed these with the soap and replaced them, the skull is to be plentifully smeared, and its cavities filled with cotton ; the whole of the skin being likewise *dressed with the arsenical soap*, is to be restored to its natural position ; the head drawn back through the neck by means of the thread attached to the mandibles ; the feathers carefully smoothed down ; the skin slightly stuffed with tow or cotton, and sewn up. A neat label having notes of the following particulars should be tied to one of the legs :—

" Native and other names ; sex, verified by dissection, if possible ; colour of the eyes, cere, legs, and fleshy parts, before fading. Date when, and place where killed."

The above notes should always be *promptly taken and attached to each specimen* immediately upon being skinned, in order to insure perfect accuracy. A number may be added to the label referring to a page in the note-book, wherein all other particulars that can be obtained should be recorded, as to habits, food, &c., and to ascertain the latter, the crop and gizzard should always be examined.

The skin may now be rolled in a strip of paper and pinned or tied moderately close to prevent the feathers being ruffled, and then placed in a safe and airy place till dry, when it may be stored in an air-tight and vermin-proof box or chest, with other skins, and camphor placed therewith, as directed for skins of mammalia.

Great care should be taken throughout to avoid cutting,

tearing, or stretching the skin, or ruffling the feathers ; and the beak and nostrils, and the scales of the legs, should be carefully preserved from injury.

Large-headed birds, such as ducks and woodpeckers will require an incision to be made down the upper part of the throat, in order to skin the skull and remove the flesh, for, it is impossible in these to draw the head through the narrow skin of the neck, which, as well as all other parts of the skin, must be carefully kept from being stretched, or it will become most unsightly, and can never be reduced to its proper size.

Before throwing away the carcase of any rare bird, two additional preparations may be made of considerable interest to the ornithologist; the first, by carefully removing the tongue and trachea, or wind pipe, cleaning them of loose integument, placing them in water a sufficient time to soak out the blood, and then pinning them on a board to dry, or, to prevent the windpipe breaking, which it is very likely to do, inserting a slender stick within it, and allowing it to dry thereon ; the second, by preserving the sternum or breast-bone of the bird, with all the smaller bones attached to it, the furcula or merry-thought, the collar and shoulder bones, and the processes which unite the sternum to the ribs. The flesh should be removed with care, and the sternum soaked in water slightly boiled, to remove the blood and flesh, and then dried. Both should be carefully labelled with the name of the bird to which they belong, or a reference to it by number. Entire skeletons of rare birds may be prepared in the same manner as those of mammalia; or, when small enough, they may be put whole into spirit until arrival at home.

REPTILES.

Reptiles of moderate size are best preserved in spirit, a portion being injected into the mouth and vent. In the largest of those thus preserved, an incision should be made in the abdomen to allow the spirit access to the intestines, previously to placing the creatures in the jar or barrel. Specimens too large to be thus disposed of, as crocodiles and large lizards, should be skinned according to the directions given for mammalia. Tortoises and turtles must have the lower shell cut or sawn from the upper, at their junction, and cut from the surrounding skin. The flesh can then be readily removed from both shells, and the head, neck, and extremities can be skinned in the usual manner. The application of arsenical soap, or preservative, must on no account be omitted.

In skinning snakes which may be inconveniently large to put in spirit, care must be taken to avoid rubbing off or loosening the scales, as well as to avoid receiving any scratch from the fangs of such as are poisonous; the virus retaining its deadly power after death, and even after long preservation.

The amphibious reptiles, as toads, frogs, newts, salamanders, &c., which undergo so many, and such remarkable transformations, should *have specimens in all the different stages of development,* from the spawn to the perfectly formed animal, preserved in spirit; and if possible, to secure identity, the different species *should be kept in separate bottles,* and all the particulars that can be obtained relating to them should be recorded in the note-book, especially the date and place of capture; and the specimens referred to by numbers marked on suitable labels.

Many remarkable species of newts and salamanders are found in Japan, particularly one very large kind—the *Sieboldia maxima*—which grows to the length of two feet. This is a very ugly creature, but very rare in European collections, and is well worth seeking for and preserving in spirit.

The eggs of reptiles should be preserved. They may be blown, or put in spirit. Particular care should be taken in ascertaining and noting the species they belong to, examples of which should also be preserved, if possible, in order to make the identification sure.

FISH.

In this, more perhaps than in any other class of animals, may the assistance of members of the Mercantile Marine be expected. Anybody can catch fish; anybody can, with little care, skin and slightly stuff them, and, with less trouble still, can preserve them in spirit or even in salt. The species are excessively numerous; the numbers of some kinds prodigious; the forms of many are very remarkable; and the beauty of others unsurpassed. *Yet fish are rarely brought home* by British collectors. Probably not fifty or even twenty species could be found at any one time in all the Natural History dealers' stores in the three kingdoms, while of birds, insects and shells thousands may certainly be obtained. Need more be said to commend this interesting class to the attention of those to whom this paper is addressed? Even the markets and those who supply them with fish may most usefully be put under contribution.

Fish as well as reptiles are best preserved in spirit, and of this more anon; but when the specimens are too large to be preserved they may be skinned. In order to prevent as much as possible the scales from being rubbed during this process, it is advisable to use some light thin substance, as old linen or cotton rags, bladder, sheet india-rubber, or even paper, to wrap the fish in, to save rubbing and chafing with the hands. This can be removed by damping when the skin is freed from the carcase. The incision for skinning may either be made down the centre of the abdomen, as in quadrupeds and birds, or it may be made midway along one side of the fish, from the pectoral fins nearly or quite to the tail. With broad-scaled or delicate fish this method has advantages; the skin of the side being stronger than that on the belly, it does not so readily tear when being sown up by the stuffer; in the case of delicate fish, and with broad-scaled ones, the loss of a few scales on *one* side is of less importance (those on the other being perfect) than on the median line of the belly.

All the flesh should, of course, be carefully removed, not only from the skin but from the base of the fins and tail and from the skull. All these parts should be well anointed with arsenical soap, or whatever preservative is used instead of it. The skin may then be very *slightly* stuffed with light material, lightly stitched up, and when thoroughly dry, wrapped in paper before being packed away, in order to prevent damage to the fins and scales, which are very easily injured.

A less troublesome process than that of skinning the entire fish is sometimes followed, namely, that of skinning very little more than one side of the fish. Make an incision from the top of the head along the back, keeping slightly on, say, the *right* side of the dorsal fin, down to the tail; continue this incision from the tail, along the belly, up to the gills. Cut away this smaller half of the skin and remove the flesh from the other; and if the head be large, cut away a portion of the thickness of this also, but leave the mouth intact. Dress the larger half of the skin with preservative, pin it on a soft board, with all the fins, as well as the tail, fully displayed, and give proper convexity to the skin by lightly inserting cotton or other soft material between it and the board. When dry, the pins may be taken out and the board and cotton removed. When viewed from the side, the absence of the other half is not noticeable, while all that is really serviceable is preserved.

Fish are very subject to *parasites*. These should be carefully sought for on the eyes, lips and gills, as well as in the liver, intestines and stomach, in which also many other creatures, preyed upon by the fish, as smaller animals of its own class, crustacea, mollusca, &c., may be found. All these should be preserved in spirit and *carefully labelled with the name of the fish from which they were taken.*

As the colours of fish are always fleeting, and often extremely beautiful, notes should be taken while the specimens are fresh, and if colored sketches can be made of rare ones, so much the better.

With reference to the preservation of fish in spirits the following points should be carefully attended to. Before immersion, a slight hole should be neatly cut in the abdomen without injuring the intestines, and a little spirit, if possible, injected therein and through the mouth and vent, light plugs of cotton being afterwards inserted in all three.

Tie to each fish a label of the date and place of capture. This may be written clearly and distinctly with a *good* pencil on stout writing paper, or on card, or best of all on parchment; or it may be written in ink, which, if allowed *to dry* before going into spirit, will not afterwards run. Where several specimens or species captured at the same time and place are put into one vessel, it will suffice to put the date and locality securely to this; but wherever any information relative to a specimen can be given, this should invariably either be affixed to it in full, or a reference to a note be attached.

Very small specimens are best preserved apart from large ones, say in pickle bottles. Thin-skinned and delicate fish should also be preserved apart from large and rough ones. All fish of any size should be separately wrapped in thin bunting, calico, or old linen, to prevent the loss of scales, and either wrapped securely, but lightly, with string, or be slightly sewn up before immersion in spirit. In order to insure preservation, it is extremely desirable, after four or five days, to draw off the spirit in which the specimens were first placed, and to substitute fresh spirit. The loss by absorption and evaporation makes this necessary. The fish, securely and separately wrapped up after having been in the first spirit, may be packed in a small barrel. The barrel must be *filled*, either with specimens, or with tow, hair, &c., to prevent tossing about; then headed up, filled with the strongest spirit obtainable, rolled, and canted to let all enclosed air escape, then filled to the bung-hole, and securely bunged up, with a piece of tin nailed over to prevent the bung getting loose. In very hot climates it may be necessary to change the spirit a second time before closing up. Much will depend upon the heat, the mass of fish to be preserved, and the strength of the spirit. Risk of damage will be lessened by putting fish into three or four small barrels, rather than into one large one of equal capacity. To prevent rolling and shaking during the time specimens are being collected, an India rubber bag, or one or more bladders, inflated with air, may be put in with the fish to keep the barrels always full, and as more fish are put in, a proportionate quantity of air can be let out.

Dr. Günther, of the British Museum, in some instructions for collecting reptiles and fish, recently issued by him, recommends for the preservation and conveyance of spirit specimens the use of square boxes made of strong tin. When *filled* with specimens, the top should be soldered on, and the spirit afterwards poured in through a hole punched in the lid until every crevice is filled, when the hole is to be covered with a small piece of tin and securely soldered. These boxes would have to be made for the purpose; they are the lightest and most compact that can be used, and if made of slightly increasing sizes, may, until wanted, be packed one within the other.

American naturalists have a modification of this plan. They use tin boxes with as large a circular hole on the top as can be made, into which a brass collar fits to receive an iron lid screwing into it, a washer of leather or gutta percha between, further aiding in preventing the escape of spirit. The advantage of these cans consists in the facility with which they can be opened and closed. Empty ammunition cans answer nearly or quite as well.

When not convenient either to skin fish, or preserve them in spirit, they may be *simply salted*. For this purpose, cut them open nearly to the back; gut them; fill them with coarse salt, and pack them in the same, with the addition of a little saltpetre.

INSECTS.

The opportunities for collecting and making observations upon insects will, probably, be as rare with members of the Mercantile Marine as those for observing and collecting the eggs of Birds. Instructions for preserving zoological specimens, however, would be very incomplete without some brief directions relative to this, the most numerous of all classes of animated beings.

The most profitable service that can be rendered will be, whenever opportunity occurs, to inquire into and secure everything illustrating the usefulness of insects to man, with a view to the possible extension of their good services. The silkmoths are a case in point. The Ailanthus silkmoth, long known to naturalists, and for centuries cultivated in China, was introduced to Europe, in 1856, by the Abbé Fantoni, a Piedmontese missionary. It is now cultivated largely and profitably in France, and, being very hardy, is also being reared in England. More than forty species of silk-producing moths have been described by naturalists; but the majority of the species are very imperfectly known, as to their food, habits, and transformations. Several of these have only been discovered within the last few years. Five of the new species are from Japan; and, as silk-producing moths are widely dispersed through the East, it is quite possible to render important service, by procuring examples of the eggs, caterpillars, cocoons, and perfect insects, of any species known to produce silk, with samples of the silk itself. A yet greater service would be performed by obtaining and carefully conveying home *living* cocoons, to hatch and breed in this country, and for the last purpose, a knowledge of the proper food-plant is most essential.*

Next to useful insects, illustrations of those which are the source of injuries to man will be worthy of attention.

Finally, the habits, transformations, and economy of Insects generally, are a most profitable field of study, whenever opportunity may occur, and illustrations of these are *well* worthy of preservation.

Butterflies, moths, and other delicate insects, may be killed with chloroform, with the vapour of ether, by holding them in the steam of a kettle, or by dipping a needle into a solution of oxalic acid, and piercing therewith the chest immediately behind the head. Butterflies may be killed also by pinching them smartly with the finger and thumb under the wings, but this is a very rough method, to be avoided when other means are possible. Very large moths should have the body opened, the contents removed, and replaced by fine cotton. Moths, butterflies, &c., should be pinned *between the wings*, with slender pins of suitable length, and stuck in *air-tight* book boxes, lined with cork; or on shallow trays, lined with cork or pith, and fitting into an *air-tight* chest; camphor, or other similar drug, being placed in each box or tray, in muslin, or other light material, to prevent minute depredators committing havoc amongst them, which they will not fail to do, unless great care and watchfulness be exercised. Great care should be taken to fasten the camphor beyond all chance of becoming loose.

Beetles may be killed instantaneously by immersion in

* For fuller particulars on this subject see a shilling pamphlet, by Lady Dorothy Neville, on the "Ailanthus Silkworm." Published at 162, Fleet-street; and "Notes on the Silk-producing Insects of India, and its adjacent countries," by Mr. F. Moore. Published in "The Technologist," for July, 1862.

A prize of 1,000 francs is offered by the Societé Impériale Zoologique d' Acclimatation, at Paris, for the acclimatation in France, or Algeria, prior to December, 1866, of any new species of moth, producing silk fit for industrial purposes. The Acclimatization Society of London is also desirous of aiding in the naturalizing in England of silk-moths, or other creatures likely to prove serviceable.

boiling water; they should afterwards be dried on a cloth, or blotting paper, and either pinned through the *right* wing-case and arranged in boxes or trays, as above directed for moths, &c., or be put in small numbers into little chip or pill-boxes, with a little cotton to keep them from shaking. Beetles, and, indeed, *all* insects, *except moths and butterflies*, may be put into spirit, which will cause immediate death, and preserve them as long as it retains its strength, to secure which, fresh spirit should be added before putting a bottle in store. Spiders and caterpillars are most easily preserved in spirit, but *can* be preserved *dry* by puncturing the abdomen, squeezing out the contents, filling it with sand and letting it remain till the skin becomes sufficiently dry, when it may be shaken out, and the specimens pinned.

Pins of various sizes, suitable for insects, may be obtained of Messrs. Edelston and Williams, Crown Court, Cheapside, London, and of Mr. Edmondson, Basnett-street, Liverpool.

Insect boxes, lined with cork, may also be procured of Mr. Edmondson, in Liverpool, and in London, of Mr. Cook, 513, New Oxford-street, from whom all other necessary entomological apparatus may be obtained. In the absence of boxes specially prepared for insects, rough ones, which will answer the purpose of conveying specimens safely home, may be made as follows :—Cut into slices about a quarter of an inch thick any good bottle corks and bungs that can be obtained, and glue them in rows, at suitable intervals, in any shallow boxes or trays that can be made to shut perfectly close.

SHELLS AND MOLLUSCOUS ANIMALS.

The following excellent instructions for collecting specimens of this very numerous and important class of animals have been extracted from a little work published by the late William Swainson, and approved by Dr. Gray :—

" *Land* Shells may be got most plentifully early in the

morning, especially in rainy weather, on shrubs and grass; the smaller kinds under moss—in the hollows of bones—under stones—in the crannies of the bark of trees, or under the moss at their roots—by the sides of ditches, and in other moist places.

" *Fresh-water* Shells are to be sought after in quiet inlets, on the sides of rivers, lakes, brooks, and canals; in ditches and ponds which are constantly full of water, and not disturbed by cattle or other means, and on the weeds and other vegetables which grow in them. To collect them, a net or tin spoon, pierced with holes, is required. The double shells, as mussels, and such like, however, mostly live on, or under, the mud.

" The *Marine* Shells are very numerous, and, according to their genera, inhabit various places.

" The cavities and surfaces of the rocks on the sea-coast afford periwinkles, limpets, sea-ears, mussels, &c. The two first kinds must be severed from the place to which they adhere, by swiftly passing a knife between them and the rock. If such of the large stones as are moveable are overturned, many sorts will be discovered sticking together on the underside; and a great variety may be found on the sea-weeds, especially after a gale, when many of these plants are thrown up by the waves.

" Such sand-banks and coral-reefs, as are for the most part overflowed by the tide at its lowest ebb, abound with thorny, and other oysters, &c.

" Under the sand and mud, often to the depth of two or three feet, live many various tribes of cockles, and other double shells, many of which spout up the water, or sink the surface of their beds by which they may be discovered; and here also, and in swamps, elephant's teeth, and other tubular shells are to be met with, the animals only of which are above the surface of the mud.

" Several kinds live on the sea-shore, about low water mark, immersed in holes which they scoop out within chalk, lime-stones, wood, &c., which must be broken or split to discover the enclosed shells. Pieces of the bed might be saved with the shells in them.

"But trawling and dredging in deep water afford the best opportunities for collecting rarities, as among the rubbish, sea-weeds, &c., which come up in the net, many curious sorts of scallops and other shells are to be got, which are not to be found near the land.

"Many shell-fish may also be procured by baiting a wicker basket, open at the ends, but gradually narrowing inwards, like a mouse-trap. It should be baited at night, and let down from the vessel when at anchor. The refuse of fish or animals will answer as a bait.

"If a bundle of straw is tied tight at one end, with a piece of meat in it, and is sunk to the bottom, many shell-fish, &c., will be found in it, if it is raised with the loose end uppermost. There should be a weight at the end to keep the straw down.

"A common swab sunk to the bottom will bring up many shells and corals.

"If the intestines of a fish are examined, many beautiful small shells will be found in them, and be easily separated after they have been for a few days in a bucket of salt-water.

"If the mud brought up by the anchor is examined, very fine shells will frequently be found in it, particularly in the eastern seas ; the lead also brings up shells.

"The natural skin or epidermis peculiar to many kinds of shells, should not on any account be taken off ; nor should the shells be touched with any corroding acid, as it spoils them.

"Shells that have been exposed on the sea-shore to the effects of sun or water, lose their colour, and are rarely worth collecting.

"It is particularly requested that no shells may be rejected, because they are common-looking, or ugly, or small."

The simplest method of killing the animals of shells is to pour *boiling* water upon them, which causes immediate death. The animals of univalve shells can then be extracted with a long bent pin, or a piece of fine wire, hooked at the end. Care should be taken to remove every particle of the animal matter of all except the very smallest kinds, and when there is a shelly lid or covering *(operculum)* to the mouth of the shell, this should be carefully put in again when dry.

Bivalve shells, as mussels, &c., must have the animal matter removed with a knife, and the two shells *tied* together; otherwise, when dry, they will gape, and be unsightly, and liable to break. The shells, when thoroughly dry, should be wrapped or packed in cotton wool, or soft paper. Very small ones may be put together in pill-boxes, or small phials, with a little cotton, to prevent shaking. All captured at one time and place should be packed together, and carefully labelled with the locality, conditions under which found, as, " under stones," " among moss," &c. ; *and (where they have been obtained by dredging) the depth in fathoms, and the nature of the bottom, whether sandy, muddy, or rocky, should be particularly named.* These last particulars are of the highest importance, not only in the study of recent conchology, but also to the geologist, as affording him hints as to the conditions under which similar kinds found in a fossil state also existed.

It is very desirable to preserve some of the specimens of shells *with the animals within them* in bottles of spirit, as it is only from the animals themselves that their true nature and relations can be accurately ascertained, as shown in the instance of the Nautilus, before spoken of. The specimens so to be preserved should be put in alive, as the spirit itself will speedily kill them.

Beside the animals bearing an external shell, there are whole families belonging to this class in which the shell is concealed within the substance of the creature, as in slugs, cuttle-fish, and squids; or is altogether wanting, as in the highly interesting nudibranchs, or naked-gilled molluscs. These should be zealously and carefully collected and preserved in spirit : the small kinds in tubes or bottles of corresponding size, and labelled as already directed.

There are very many highly interesting molluscous animals which are found floating on the surface of the sea. These should be collected by means of a net consisting of a ring of iron, or a strong wooden hoop of a barrel, having a bag about eighteen or twenty inches deep, made of bunting. Three pieces of cord, about twenty inches long, should be tied to the ring at equal distance, and the ends tied together to a long line, with which the whole should be towed from the boat or ship on the water, so as to skim its surface. The net should be frequently examined, and the captures, however minute, put into small phials of spirit, and labelled with the date, and latitude and longitude.

Gulf-weed should be closely examined for specimens of these floating molluscs, which are great prizes to conchologists.*

CRUSTACEA.

All Crustacea (lobsters, crabs, shrimps, &c.) are *best* preserved in spirit, which, of course, immediately kills them. Specimens too large for this method should have all the flesh carefully removed. Access to it may be obtained by removing or loosening the upper shell in crabs, in lobsters, cray-fish, &c. ; an incision may be made for this purpose down the middle of the under side. The claws must be taken off at the joints to extract the flesh if it cannot be removed by cutting through the integument on the inner side of the joints. If taken off, they must be carefully replaced. The whole of the

---

* Those persons who have the slightest inclination for studying shells should possess themselves of a copy of Woodward's " Manual of Mollusca," published by Weale, 59, High Holborn, London. Price 6s. 6d. This most admirable book is a library of itself upon the animals of which it treats.

shell should, subsequently, be immersed in spirit for a short time, or else be anointed internally with arsenical soap, to prevent the attacks of insects. This class of animals is very numerous, and will well repay collecting and studying. The small kinds, however minute, should be assiduously sought for and preserved.

ANNELIDS, OR WORMS.

Under the lowly designation of worms are included a considerable variety of creatures, which, though less frequently studied and collected, perhaps, than any others, are well worthy of attention. Many are really very beautiful when seen in a living state. The nereids, which burrow in sand or mud, when swimming reflect brilliant iridescent tints, and make their way through the water by a series of most graceful curves, which no one who is fortunate enough to see them can fail to admire. So little are they sought after, that though beautiful specimens, a foot in length, are to be found buried deep in the shores of the Mersey, they are almost as little known as if they inhabited the antipodes ; and the exhibition of specimens in the Aquaria, at the Free Public Museum, never fails to elicit the admiration of all who see them. Other members of the tribe form tubes of sand and shell, by means of their flexible and extensive feelers, working like so many miniature elephants' trunks ; other kinds spread out beyond the leathery tube in which they live, a beautiful spiral disc, like a plume of delicate feathers, which they instantly retract on the slightest alarm ; others, again, form calcareous tubes, the mouth of which they close against all intruders by a most exquisitely contrived stopper. These are examples of a portion only of the numerous class of Annelids. They are to be sought for under stones, or buried more or less deep in sand or mud ; their whereabouts being generally betrayed by some orifice, or depression, or by castings thrown up out of their holes. Those which burrow must be dug for with a spade or three-pronged fork, deeply and quickly, or they will evade pursuit. Immersion in water to cleanse them is necessary to display their beauty. Those forming hard tubes generally attach them to shells, stones, &c. All these creatures can only be preserved in spirit; and those kinds forming tubes should be preserved *in them undisturbed*; or at least some example should be so saved. It is not always easy to prevent the animals slipping out; when they do so, the tube should be put into the bottles with them.

STAR-FISH AND SEA URCHINS, SEA ANEMONES AND ZOOPHYTES, ACALEPHS OR JELLY FISHES, CORALS AND SPONGES.

With the exception of the Jelly Fish, which are best secured by the towing net, while swimming near the surface, all the above creatures are to be procured by searching along the shore at low tides, and by the use of the trawl and dredge.

Star-fish may be preserved dry; very small kinds without any other preparation than a brief immersion in spirit. All large Star-fish should have the flesh removed. To do this, cut from the mouth to the lip of each arm, on the under side, with a pair of scissors stout enough to divide the internal frame-work. With a bluntish knife, the fleshy matter may then be easily removed from the centre and from each arm. Soak the skin in spirit, but very briefly, for fear of loss of color, and pin out the specimen on a piece of soft-board and place it in the sun, or before a fire, or in a strong current of air, so that it may dry rapidly. When thoroughly dry, fold in thin paper.

Echini, or Sea-urchins, are more difficult to preserve dry, especially those with very large spines. The flesh must be removed through the mouth on the under side; cut the skin surrounding this, and scoop out the flesh, but leave in the loose internal framework. Soak in spirit for a short time, and dry as above.

Specimens of as many kinds as possible of Star-fish and Sea-
urchins should be wrapped up separately and preserved in
spirit, dried specimens being insufficient for the examination
of all parts of their structures.

Sea Anemones are difficult to preserve satisfactorily. If
possible, cut away with a hammer and chisel a small piece of
the rock to which they are attached; place them in salt-water
until they expand; then suddenly transfer them to spirit while
so expanded. When dead, it will be well to fold each specimen that is so attached in linen, to prevent damage from
chafing, rendered more probable than usual by the piece of
adhering rock.

Allied to the Anemones, though very much lighter and more
graceful in form, are those beautiful, delicate, little, slender
shrub-like objects so familiar to all who visit the sea-coast at
low tides, where, though not frequently met with attached to
the rocks, they are yet found in great abundance left in heaps
by the receding tide. Careful examination will show to the
naked eye, in many cases, that these objects are serrated like
the teeth of a ,saw. The use of a pocket lens will reveal
the fact that each of these serrations is a little cavity, and if
placed under a microscope, in a little water, when fresh from
the sea, each cavity will be found to have its own tiny occu-
pant, whose structure and movements it will be most interesting to watch. A few observations like these will enable any
person not previously familiar with these little creatures, to
distinguish them from sea-weeds, with which they are not
seldom confounded by ordinary observers. These *zoöphytes*
should be carefully collected and preserved. For this purpose,
preference should be given to those found attached at the base,
to rocks, stones, &c. These will be alive. They should be
carefully removed from whatever they may be fixed to, and
plunged immediately into small phials of spirit, which, if
neatly done, will generally result in the little occupants being

killed protruding from their cells, thus affording the best means of examining them, when living specimens cannot be obtained.

When procured by the dredge, it is less necessary to restrict one's self to rooted specimens, as those brought up will probably be living, having been torn from their hold by the dragging of the dredge. Many of these objects are very dwarfish in size; minute specimens, therefore, found on small stones, shells, &c., should be saved, and may be put, shell and all, in spirit.

The Acalephs, or Jelly-fish tribe, vary greatly in size, from that of a pea, to monsters of a foot or two in diameter. They can only be preserved in fluid; and of fluids, *spirit* is most generally available. Into this they should be placed as soon as possible after capture; the small specimens, which should be carefully sought for, chiefly by the *towing net*, being put into bottles of proportionate size.

Corals, especially the smaller kinds, and in seas where they are neglected, are well worth collecting; and the preservation in spirit of small specimens, or fragments of large ones, fresh from the sea, with the animal attached, is worth attempting. Of sponges, there is a very great variety; and but little labour is necessary in order to their preservation. They should be carefully packed in soft material when dry.

It is most important that all the various kinds of specimens, here alluded to, should be fully and accurately labelled with the time and place of capture, and any additional information that can be gathered should either be added to the label, or entered at length in the note-book.

DIATOMACEÆ, AND OTHER MINUTE OBJECTS.

The following instructions are drawn up by the Society of Microscopists of Manchester. The objects to which they relate are exceedingly numerous, both in individuals and species. They will well repay the trouble of collecting, and of any time that can be devoted to their study. A small microscope will be of great service in examining them, and will prove a never-ending source of interest and delight.

" These minute forms are found in all waters, but the most interesting species are those found in salt water, especially shallow lagoons, salt-water marshes, estuaries of rivers, pools left by the tide, &c.

" Their presence in any quantity is always shewn by the colour they impart to the aquatic plants and sea-weeds to which they are found attached, and if found on the mud, which is very frequently the case, they impart to it also a yellowish brown colour approaching to black brown if in great numbers.

" This brownish pellicle, if carefully removed with a spoon (without disturbing the mud) will be found very pure. Capital gatherings of Diatomaceæ might be obtained by carefully scraping the brown-coloured layer from mooring posts, and piles of wharfs and jetties.

" In clear running ditches, the plants and stones have often long streamers of yellowish brown slimy matter attached to them, which is generally diatomaceous.

" When found in large quantities on the mud, the layer is often covered with bead-like bubbles of oxygen. This often detaches them from the bottom and buoys them to the surface, where they form a dense brown scum, which is blown to leeward in large quantities, and presents the general appearance of dark-coloured yeast.

" In this form it may be collected in abundance, often quite free from particles of sand and other impurities.

" Good and rare species have been obtained from the stomachs of oysters, scallops and other shell-fish inhabiting deep water.

" The sea-cucumbers (Holothuridæ) found so frequently in southern latitudes, ought to contain many species.

" These animals might be simply dried and preserved just as found, and the contents of the stomach afterwards obtained by dissection.

" The Noctilucæ, which cause the phosphorescence in the sea, are diatom-feeders, and may be caught in large quantities in a fine gauze towing-net.

" The Ascidians, found attached to oyster shells and stones from deep water, have yielded excellent gatherings.

" The Salpæ, often noticed in warm latitudes floating on the surface of the sea, and assuming chain and other like forms, ought to be bottled up for examination. These Salpæ are well-known diatom-feeders.

" Deep sea soundings ought to be preserved, especially from great depths, and are often exclusively diatomaceous. Sea-weed from rocks ought to be preserved, especially the smaller species, and if covered with a brown furriness, so much the better.

" Very rare species have been found in immense quantities in the Arctic and Atlantic regions, by melting the '*pancake ice*,' which is often found discoloured of a brown tint in consequence of the great numbers of these minute beings.

" The sea is often observed to be discoloured by brownish patches. The discoloured water (or '*spawn*,' as it is called) should be collected, filtered through cotton-wool, and the brown residue preserved.

" When a fine impalpable dust is observed to be falling at sea, it ought to be collected from the folded sails and other places where it lodges. This may yield Diatomaceæ which, from the method of collecting, would be highly interesting to examine.

" The roots of the various species of Mangrove (*Rhizophora*) which form impenetrable barriers along the salt-water rivers and estuaries in the tropical parts of Africa, Australia, the Eastern Archipelago, &c., are found frequently covered with a brown mucous slime, said to be very rich in Diatomaceæ.

" When the Diatomaceæ are collected from any of the above-mentioned sources they may be at once transferred to small bottles, or the deposit may be partially dried and wrapped up in pieces of paper or tinfoil. When placed in bottles, a few drops of spirits added will keep them sweet.

" In all cases it is essential to keep the gatherings separate and distinct, and that the locality whence obtained be written on each package.

" All shells and stones from deep water which are covered with sea-weed ought to be preserved, as affording interesting and little known species. The rougher these are the better, and on no account ought they to be washed."

Soundings (especially if brought up with *soap* instead of *fatty matter*) may very readily be preserved by sticking them on to pieces of paper, with a memorandum of the date, depth, and latitude and longitude, &c. Ordinary envelopes will answer very well for the purpose, as the soundings when dry may be put either on the inner side of the envelope or be attached to a separate piece of paper and slipped in like a letter.

The sea-cucumbers, ascidians, salpæ, &c., mentioned above, should be assiduously collected *for their own sake*, as well as for the reasons here given.

TRAWLING AND DREDGING.

In water not too deep for the use of a trawl, large numbers of marine animals of all kinds, fish, crustacea, shells, star-fish, &c., &c., may be most readily obtained. Large collections may be made in a short time and with little trouble. Trawling is therefore strongly recommended.

For procuring small specimens, such as would escape through the wide meshes of the trawl, *a dredge is most desirable*. Indeed for deep water this only is available for collecting ground specimens. Dredging is therefore also most strongly recommended.

Dredges may be procured in Liverpool of Mr. Edmondson, Basnett Street, or of Mr. Finchett, Button Street, Whitechapel; and in London of Mr. Highley, 74, Dean Street, Soho.*

As the special object in dredging is to procure specimens from the sea-bottom, a quantity of mud and sand is often brought up. A small brass sieve is therefore requisite, by which to sift the minute specimens from the mud, &c., by pouring water through the sieve. The specimens so obtained may be put into small bottles of spirit and labelled with the depth in fathoms from which obtained, nature of the sea bottom, and lat. and long., as before directed.

Where the sea-bed is covered with coral, large masses may be detached by means of a strong drag-hook, and many living creatures may be found sheltered and hiding between the branches. These should be carefully extracted, put in bottles of spirits, and labelled accordingly.

Whenever opportunities occur of examining the *sea-beach and the shores* of tidal rivers, they should be made the most of. Proceeding thither as the tide goes out, and working gradually down to extreme low water-mark, a great variety of specimens may be obtained which are not to be procured either by trawling or dredging, as different depths of the sea bottom have their own peculiar kinds of living creatures. All stones and pieces of rock that it is possible to move should be turned over, as creatures of all kinds either attach themselves to the under side, or bury in the sand or mud beneath. Wherever there is any depression in the sand, &c., some living creature is probably buried beneath; but, as many of them burrow very rapidly or already have deep holes excavated into which to retreat on the first symptom of danger, considerable dexterity and quickness are necessary to secure them.

* It is difficult to give instructions for making a dredge without having a wood-cut illustration to refer to. Those who may not be able to procure one ready-made will find a good figure and description in Woodward's " Manual of the Mollusca," (before referred to) at pages 428 and 429, together with other information most useful to dredgers, and one or more dredges can always be seen at the Liverpool Free Public Museum.

All possible search should be made as the tide recedes, and the lower it falls the richer and rarer will the harvest of specimens generally be. Wrack, and sea-weed of all kinds, should be examined for specimens lurking therein. A basket with wide-mouthed bottles, and a spade to dig for the animals which burrow, are necessary accompaniments when hunting the shore and beach.

SPIRIT SPECIMENS.

As repeatedly mentioned in the preceding pages, it is extremely desirable, at least once, to change the spirit in all bottles, jars, &c., in which specimens are preserved, in order to make good the loss by absorption and evaporation. Considerable care is requisite in finally fastening up the bottles, as bungs in particular are often made of inferior cork. The following method is recommended by Mr. Wm. Stimpson, late naturalist to the United States' Expedition to the North Pacific Ocean, as having been adopted for all his smaller vessels with eminent success. Take some ordinary calico or linen, soak it in common bees' wax melted by the fire, and let it dry. Cut from this a circular piece, put it over the mouth of the bottle, and drive it in tight with the cork or bung. Cut a larger piece, and tie it tightly over the cork *and the head of the bottle*. The wax will adhere sufficiently to prevent any further escape of spirit. The same gentleman also recommends the use of plaster of Paris for effectually closing large jars. Some kind of lid or cover is necessary, but upon this a little plaster of Paris, mixed with water, may be easily run, and it will dry immediately and form a perfectly air-tight covering. Care of course should be taken to prevent it getting in among the specimens.

Glass bottles containing spirit specimens may be easily and safely packed by wrapping them well with hay or other soft material, and then in paper. In this manner they can be stowed away (corks uppermost) in a box or chest without fear of damage.

AQUARIA.

The establishment of an Aquarium on board ship may appear at first sight to be difficult or impossible. Really it is not so, at least on a small scale. Glass globes, such as are ordinarily used for gold-fish, answer very well for this purpose Take a circular piece of wood an inch thick ; to this attach four small cords of twelve or fourteen inches long, bind their loose ends to a metal eye, place a globe on this stand within the four cords, hang it to a hook in the cabin ceiling, and it will swing as safely as a lamp. In this way globes of the kind above-named, containing living specimens, have been conveyed four times across the Atlantic by Capt. Mortimer in the ship "Florida," without being broken or damaged. A double object may be attained by the establishment of small aquaria of this kind : they afford the opportunity of closely studying various interesting living objects, and of importing them to England.

With the multitude of ships and steamers constantly arriving in our ports, and the quickness of their passage as compared with former times, it is not a little surprising that so few living exotic creatures have been imported by this method, either for purposes of naturalization or to supply the demand for interesting specimens for aquaria.

One or two hints may be useful to those disposed to make an attempt. *Never try to bring more than two or three specimens, and these of small size, in a single globe.* Three fish as large as minnows would be quite as many as could live long together in such limited space. Hang the globe in the coolest part of the vessel, in a shady place. Strong light and warmth are very prejudicial. Draw off with a clean siphon, or other means, a portion of the water, daily if possible, and supply its place with more. A little fine sand, washed free from anything that will obscure the water, may in the outset be put in the bottom of the globe, or, instead of sand, a little extremely fine shingle may be used. This affords opportunities for groping and hiding which many creatures indulge in.

The floating shell-fish of the ocean, shell-fish of other kinds, small crabs, &c.; and small specimens of the numberless, beautiful species of fish, beside more minute objects, would afford ample material for study, and would be received with delight in England.

To import *large* specimens it will be necessary to keep them in a bucket, or barrel, with plenty of air playing over it, a daily change of water, and a shady situation.

Frequent change of a portion, at least, of the water in the globe aquaria will generally afford sufficient nutrition for their occupants. If, however, feeding should be necessary, a minute crumb or two of ship-biscuit may be dropped in the water occasionally, for fishes. For crabs, prawns, &c., a tiny piece of fish may be placed in the water for half an hour; but on no account should food of any kind be allowed to remain, as it will contaminate the water more than any other cause. Specimens that may die in the aquaria should, for the same reason, be immediately removed. The best criterion of the well-doing of an aquarium is the state of the water. If this, when undisturbed, is quite clear, all is as it should be. If it be at all obscure or discolored, it should be immediately changed.

METHOD FOR COLLECTING AND STUDYING DESIRABLE.

In order to make the most profitable use of such time and labour as may be expended upon the subjects referred to in these pages, it is strongly recommended to those who are at all earnest in the matter, *to determine upon some method of conducting their researches.* It is not to be expected that any persons will attempt to study deeply or collect largely, all the classes of animals that have been here referred to. Some more restricted plan will be generally necessary; and it will be better, probably, in every way, that the attention should be directed chiefly to one branch of the subject; though not necessarily to the entire exclusion of all others. For instance, fish may be made the principal object of attention. Whatever time may be available for scientific pursuits, may be devoted chiefly to the capture and study of this class of animals. All those met with on any one voyage, may be noted, information obtained relating to them, and possibly several specimens preserved. A list may be made out towards the end of the voyage; and the notes copied, with references given to such specimens as have been obtained. If the names are not known, they can be referred to by numbers. Search might be made, while at home, in Natural History books in public or private libraries, to obtain the scientific names, and to learn what is already recorded about them; the assistance of some naturalist may be obtained, or the paper, as it is, might be submitted to some Natural History society; if in Liverpool, to the *Literary and Philosophical Society.* Or the sailor student, if sailing again, or continually to the same port, may continue his observations and add to his notes and his specimens; or even if sailing to other countries, the same class of animals may continue to be the objects of his attention.

By such means as the above, he is certain, sooner or later, to accumulate valuable knowledge, which, if published, can scarcely fail to aid in the furtherance of science; and to lead him to do this is the great object for which this paper is prepared.

Another method may be suggested. A captain trading regularly to one port may very properly extend his observations to many or all the classes of animals to be met with in his repeated voyages; and in time his list of specimens observed and captured, and his notes thereon, cannot fail to be of interest to naturalists.

In fact those scientific publications which are devoted to the furtherance of Natural History, contain a large proportion of papers such as would result from either of the above methods.

The pleasure which is invariably experienced in the study of natural objects would be considerably increased by such methodical working. When a man is able to add a fresh species to his list, it is done with no small amount of satisfaction; and the monotony of a dull voyage cannot but be considerably relieved by such an occurence. Moreover in comparing the list of his own captures in any particular class of animals, with the published lists of species known to exist, he will not fail to find in it many deficiences. This will lead him to search more carefully, in order to obtain the species that are wanting; and he will probably succeed in obtaining many which otherwise he would never have met with. In all probability a few will still be lacking, and he will be led to take a deeper interest in studying the distribution of species, the limits of their range, and the conditions essential to their existence. No more appropriate or more interesting subject of research can be taken up by the Mercantile Marine.

USEFUL ELEMENTARY BOOKS.

" The Animal Kingdom" of Baron Cuvier. Edited by Dr. Carpenter and J. O. Westwood, Esq. Orr and Co., London, 1854. 1 vol., large octavo, £1 1s.

This work contains a general and connected account of all classes of the animal kingdom.

" The Pictorial Museum of Animated Nature." Cox, London. 2 vols., folio, £1 16s.

This work contains nearly 4,000 woodcuts, which alone would suffice approximately to name large numbers of animals, whether vertebrate or invertebrate.

" The English Cyclopædia." By Charles Knight. *Natural History Division*. 4 vols., price £2. Bradbury and Evans, London, 1854—1856.

This goes more fully into the scientific characters and groups of animals than either of the above. It is a most useful and valuable work.

Woodward's "Manual of the Mollusca." Weale, London, 1856. 1 vol., 12mo. Indispensable to all collectors of shells. Price 6s. 6d.

Darwin's "Naturalist's Voyage round the World." Murray, London. 1 vol., 12mo, 9s.

A charming book, which cannot fail to fascinate and instruct all who read it, and to inculcate habits of observation.

"The Microscope and its Revelations." By W. B. Carpenter, M.D. Churchill, London, 1856. 1 vol. 12mo, 12s. 6d.

Most serviceable to all who use the microscope, and study the objects to which it is applicable.

"Lardner's Cabinet Cyclopædia : Birds," by W. Swainson. 2 vols. 9s. "Fishes, Amphibians, and Reptiles," by the same. 2 vols. 9s.

These volumes will be found very useful for the particular subjects on which they treat; though the writer's *theory of arrangement* has few followers. For the most generally adopted arrangement of fish, see

"Encyclopædia Britannica," 8th edition, vol 12, 1856, article Ichthyology. The two parts containing this can be had for 12s.

"Natural History of the European Seas." By Messrs. Edward Forbes and Godwin-Austen. Van Voorst, London, 1859. 12mo, 6s.

A suggestive book for Mediterranean voyagers.

AIDS FOR COLLECTING.

The following simple outfit will enable any one to make large collections of specimens :—

A dredge.

A towing net.

Glass bottles, such as empty pickle and preserve bottles; the wider in the mouth the better.

Smaller glass bottles, such as homœopathic bottles, or bottles of similar size, made out of glass tubing, and fitted with corks.

One or two pairs of small forceps, for picking up minute objects.

Pill boxes of various sizes.

A good supply of spirit.*

Ditto   salt.

Alum will also be useful for large skins.

Arsenical soap, 3 or 4lbs., for skins of quadrupeds, birds, reptiles, and fish.

Bees-wax, calico, and plaster of Paris.

A pocket lens, for examining small objects.

A small microscope would be a most useful addition, well repaying the cost, by the greater power it gives of examining the most minute specimens.

Bottles made from glass tubing are exceedingly serviceable for the isolation and preservation of small specimens. They may be had of Mr. Evans, Cleveland square, Liverpool. Very neat bottles, of a larger range of sizes, are made from glass tubing expressly for naturalists, by Mr. Wadsworth, 17, Upperhead row, Leeds, and will be found extremely useful.

Pill and chip boxes may be procured from Mr. Jackson, dealer in druggists' sundries, Cleveland square, Liverpool.

RECIPE FOR ARSENICAL SOAP.

Camphor	5 ounces
Arsenic, in powder	2 pounds
White soap	2 pounds
Salts of Tartar	12 ounces
Lime, in powder	4 ounces

Cut the soap in thin small slices, as thin as possible; put them in a pot over a gentle fire, with very little water, taking care to stir it often with a wooden spoon: when it is well melted, put in the salts of tartar and powdered chalk. Take it off the fire, add the arsenic, and triturate the whole gently. Lastly, put in the camphor, which must first be reduced to powder in a mortar, by the help of a little spirits of wine; mix the whole well together. This paste ought then to have the consistence of flour paste. Put it into glazed earthen pots,

* Methylated spirit, of full strength, answering every purpose, may be purchased, free of duty, at certain druggist's and other shops, at a cost of about 4s. to 5s. per gallon.

taking care to put a ticket on each, labelled " POISON." The three first ingredients in the above recipe may be used if the others cannot readily be obtained.

When it is to be used, put the necessary quantity into a preserve pot, dilute it with a little cold water, or, better still, with spirit, rub it with a small brush until it has the consistence of cream ; cover this pot with a lid of pasteboard, in the middle of which bore a hole for the handle of the brush.

This preparation is the most generally used for the preservation of skins of quadrupeds, birds, reptiles, and fish, and is to be freely applied with the brush, immediately after skinning, on the fleshy side of the skin. As it is a troublesome and unpleasant task to make up the prescription, it is advisable to get it done by some trustworthy druggist.